Of Omens That Flitter

Karen Kelsay

Dear Julie,
Thankyou for your friendship & help in the past! I hope we can meet this year. All the best, Karen

ISBN: 978-1-945917-26-4

Printed in the United States of America

Cover Design by Karen Kelsay
Cover photograph by Les Pickstock
Starlings and Eclipse at New Brighton
Attribution for Licensing:
https://wiki.creativecommons.org/wiki

Also by Karen Kelsay:

Lavender Song
In Spite of Her
Song of the Bluebell Fairy
A Fist of Roots
Somewhere Near Evesham
Dove on a Church Bench
Amytis Leaves Her Garden

"Making other books jealous since 2004"

Big Table Publishing Company
Boston, MA
www.bigtablepublishing.com

Acknowledgments

Measure: "To Lucette in a Field"

Boston Literary Magazine: "On the British Riviera," "Draining the Cup," "Evil Eye," "Atomic Tiki Man"

Fire in the Pasture: "How to Break a Northern Spell," "Sunset by the Oak"

Trinacria: "An Evening in May," "Pastoral to the Midlands," "Final Word," "Time Bomb," "The Courtship Hour," "Of Omens That Flitter," "Finding the Powerham Sprite," "Whispers of Dawlish," "A Californian Views a British Soap Opera," "A Troubled Lot," "Thoughts on a Step," "Hard Hat Diver"

Life and Legends: "A Cemetery in Castle Coombe," "Much from Little"

The Road Not Taken: "Lady of Shalott," "An Expatriates' Message," "Flat-screened"

Segullah: "Winter Lullaby"

Angle, Journal of Poetry: "Crossing the Divide," "Sargent Mockingbird"

Mezzo Cammin: "Drama in the Garden," "Mariana," "Gathering Moss"

The Lyric: "Surprise Possession," "Anywhere"

Kin Poetry Journal: "In the Smoky Mountains"

Red Fez: "Parrotfish"

The Nervous Breakdown: "Superchild"

Wilderness House Literary Review: "Draining the Cup," "The Courtship Hour," "Needlepoint in Blue"

The Touch: Journal of Healing: "Gathering Moss"

The Raintown Review: "Time Bomb"

Wilderness Interface Zone: "Winter in England," "Seaside at Eighty"

Verse Wisconsin: "The Tortoise and the Hare"

The Foliate Oak: "Kissing Gate," "The Courtship Hour"

Pennsylvania Review: "Seaside at Eighty"

String Poet "Outlooks," "Quiet Flame"

The Adroit Journal: "How to Break a Northern Spell"
World Riot: "Atomic Tiki Man"
14x14: "Photo Prayer"
Toasted Cheese Literary Journal: "Drawing in the Sheets"
Willow's Wept Review: "Kissing Gate"
Millers Pond: "Sara Orangetip Butterfly"
Pirene's Fountain: "Summer in Italy"
Red Lion SQ: "Violet"
Grey Sparrow: "La Sierra 1942," "Lament of the Leaves"
Flutter: "Tumbleweed"
Ink Sweat and Tears: "Eyeball Prayer"
Leaf Garden Press: "Breakfast at Las Brisas"
Linnet's Wings: "British Guy"
Triggerfish Critical Review: "Autumn Ambivalence"
Nomad's Choir: "The Old Racer"
Joyful: "Somewhere in Evesham"
The Flea: "An Expatriate's Message," "Winter in England"
Lucid Rhythms: "Dawn's Dobro"
The New Formalist: "Seaside at Eighty," "Kissing Gate"
Better than Starbucks: "Compositions by the River Dee,"
    "A Californian Views British Soap Operas," "Home Décor,"
    "Winter Lullaby," "Recognition"

Table of Contents

Spirits Here and There

Of Omens That Flitter

A flock of starlings smudge the autumn sky.
The birds swoop high and low, just like the trills
of flutes, and shift their plumage as they fly—
elusive patterns form above the hills.

The ancient Romans had an explanation:
Through movements of the birds the gods would hint
of future things. The birds, in their migration,
merge and split, and leave their dancing print

against the mystic heavens. You're the same.
You shift your course abruptly without fear,
like whirling smoke from some unnoticed flame;
then flitter through the night and disappear

in silence, with a swift and downward roll
no prophecy of augurs can control.

To Lucette, in a Field

We left to find your gravesite early morning;
mild skies were feathered robin-blue, with clouds
that nested on the rims of New York's hills,
like little ghosts tucked up in filmy shrouds.

We navigated through old Millerton,
to fields along the crest of Winchell Mountain's
coiling road, and found a sea of headstones
ascending from the grass like tilted fountains.

Your parents and five siblings all sleep here.
You were the last, according to the date,
to make your bed beneath a broken marker:
Lucette Aldrich, the youngest one of eight.

In patchwork fields, upstate, along this border,
I visualize you visiting this place.
The calmness in the air—the lulling oaks—
old liaisons that web and interlace

their roots to rock and cradle kin below.
Through earth's frail nursing blanket of decay
posterity and ancients are anointed
transcending past the grief, the bark, the clay.

Thoughts on a Step

Old step, cut from the local quarry stones,
allowing laity into the nave,
where stained glass windows, bathed in jewel-tones,
depict the Savior rising from the grave—

you're set beneath these massive gothic doors,
where people stand to view celestial walls,
examine intricate mosaic floors,
and Bishops' tombs, oak pulpits, choir stalls.

For centuries, these structures have remained
safeguarded in immaculate condition;
except for you—stone step—concaved and stained,
worn down without a drop of recognition.

But still my camera's eye has caught your worth,
revealed in what you're lacking. Smoothed by feet
that shuffle in commemorating birth,
mortality, and marriage. You complete

your testimony from this lowly station:
step on me, and rise to exaltation.

Recognition

Death is the straight-faced man who stares far off
as if his job requires a solemn look,
if you were here its certain you would scoff
at all our nervous chatter. We've no book

to guide us through the things that we must do.
Your wife seems ill-prepared, and wears a frown.
We know this cannot be the end of you—
one plastic box, beneath the sod, deep down.

Flat-screened

She had a dream her husband came to chat;
he floated by the closet near the bed,
remarking how his clothes and favorite hat
no longer occupied the shelves. She said:

I didn't know that you were coming back!
He slipped down through the hallway, searched the place
where all his books were kept, there was no stack.
A deep frown etched its way across his face.

Inside the living room he turned bright red,
a flat screen on the wall ensnared his eyes.
You're in the money now that I am dead!
At that, she sweetly whispered her good bye:

I've loved the chance to see you once again
now please be good and go back where you've been.

On Finding Great Witley Church

We saw your massive golden dome from down
below, a baroque body oddly out
of place. I snapped your picture by the brown
limbs hanging near the roadside fence, devout

old guards, one hundred years had left behind.
We leaned across your speckled balustrades
beside the river, where worn paths entwined
and crisscrossed beside watery cascades.

Then, hiking grassy slopes around the charred
magnificent old court, adjacent to
your holy place, we found a heavy door.
Surprised at how we easily slipped through,

we scramble in like heathens, unaware.
Inside were angels winged with elegance.
Subdued by stained glass, carvings, heaven's air,
we marveled at your ancient relevance.

The pious moment passed, and then I thought
of all the souls who sat within your pews;
the offerings and sadness that they brought.
Your wood grain's worn, as if it might transfuse

into a blemished song, or ancient phrase,
that mutely sings of suffering and praise.

Winter Lullaby

It's always in the violet hour you call,
when dusk spreads infant-smooth across the skies,
and winter teeters on the wings of fall.
The poplars change to gold and improvise.

In spite of chill, the memory of you warms.
Unpunctual star, kind winter brings you near,
to break you from your listlessness—transforms
that vagrant whisper I can barely hear

to incandescent words; the subtle burn
of maple leaves to red, a flame of thought
that gives the seasoned birch a breathless turn,
as random dreams within its twigs are caught.

Finding the Powderham Sprite

I sensed her by the fallow deer that fed
upon the oak leaves near the sea, and then
around the flooded estuary bed
where egrets hid between large willows. When

a heron waded through the narrow pond
and mingled with the geese, I almost saw
her cherry lips flash like a regal wand,
or damselfly, who quietly withdraws

when humans catch a glimpse. I know she's here
to gather peacock-butterflies and shells,
until thin moonbeams slowly draw her near
and ghostly forms ring silent vesper bells.

Photo Prayer

When cataracts form clouds across my eyes
like fog that settles on the coastal skies
and creaky knees require a wooden cane
to navigate my walk across the lane,
please help me not relinquish vanity
to illnesses or pain. Just swaddle me
in classic silk pajamas, sleek and black,
with little velvet shoes, no flannel sack
to drape around my bones, or pink housecoat
with fuzzy slippers skimming like a boat
across the kitchen floor. I'll take a chain
of gold, Ann Taylor slacks. Let me abstain
from wearing spongy curlers that cause laughs
when children see me in old photographs.

Whispers of Dawlish

Beside the bank where black swans often lie
in twos, beneath wild fruit trees near the stream,
and Chinese geese move single file across
the water like a strand of flags that gleam

with little angled feather tips of light;
I heard her speak. It was a quiet voice,
like summer clouds that weep along low hills
of poplar groves then peacefully rejoice

in finding laurel blooms. A haunting voice,
that sifted from another time, to leave
a secret song before the night was due
and tuck it into twilight's bell-shaped sleeve

where it might dissipate. Beside the bank,
where black swans often lie in twos, a word
clings to an apple on the bough. Sometimes
when breezes lift the branches it is heard.

Violet

Husband, I want to ripen into
a woman like your mother,
one who wiggles an arm
into the nook of a son's elbow,
feet twisting obscure angles
across frosty streets, refusing a cane.
Whose only hope from tipping
over in the lane with a dizzy spell,
is not a pill, but a bag
of hard candies to keep her upright.
A stiff-upper-lip kind of lady,
who jeers at heart attacks
and broken hips, and raises hell
when trapped in a ward with *old people.*
One who still makes tea each
morning over the burner, even though
she catches her sleeves on fire.
A woman with no riches but a few
baubles of costume jewelry
and collection of miniature brass
animals, given her one Mother's Day,
that glint in sun like a row
of diamonds.

An Evening in May

I wonder what you're up to, now, my friend.
Does springtime find you nattering away
to rabbits in the yard? Did you attend
the stragglers on that sycamore? Today,

I thought about how often you took walks
along the hedgerows, where within the light,
thin filtered rays like golden-spindled stalks,
defined the darkening edges of the night.

White daisies sprang up all around this place,
the lawn seemed rich and full, deep green, but when
a cloud disguised the brilliant Queen Anne's Lace,
the evening's dullness settled in again.

Final Word

He says that he cannot believe in God,
it's asinine to scrape, and bow, and pray.
There is no evidence; to plead and prod
an unseen entity is childish play.

He worships science, medicine, the things
concrete in nature, nothing more or less.
There are no miracles. He won't pull strings
to get a pass when he is in distress.

Each diagnosis points to his demise—
these doctors are just human. Big surprise.

Cemetery in Castle Combe

We wander through a graveyard near the church,
where only leaves assemble on the mounds,
and ivy finds salvation beside tombs.
Two grosbeaks forage insects by the grounds.

Faint epitaphs are difficult to read,
worn birth and death dates mark the vanished pride
of men who lived one hundred years ago.
On random plots we make a bona fide

endeavor to decipher phantom words.
Why do we care? These ancient souls are not
our dead. Yet, threads of curiosity
have drawn us to this wild, forsaken lot

where lichen spreads its solace, like a mother,
obscuring names of father, child, or brother.

Sara Orangetip Butterfly

You could have folded naturally
like a paper triangle, and slipped
into death's pocket—
if you weren't so beautiful.

June's mustard fields and streams
still watch for you. Verbena's purple bloom
has missed your wing. Who captured
you in mid-flight

and pinned you to this board,
forcing you to fly throughout the ages
with your elegance exposed?

Crossing the Divide

We knew beforehand we would put you down
on Wednesday evening. So we made a pact:
to spend two days inside the house. You found
a windowsill, remained aloof, and backed

against the smudgy glass behind my dresser—
with space enough for you, but not for us.
And I considered it to be a lesser
evil than a darker place. I'd fuss,

extend a finger, stroke your ear, and speak.
But with each touch you'd turn your head, withdraw.
The contact, causing pain (prognosis bleak).
Distance, was the cruel unwritten law.

You woke me up the night before you died,
to lick my face. Then, moved away and stirred
a little, several inches from my side.
And for a full five minutes, loudly purred.

Now, looking back (it's only been a week),
your gesture seems a selfless, sweet, good bye,
the way you pressed your nose against my cheek,
the night before we scheduled you to die.

Dawn's Dobro

I found your melody inside the night;
it lulled me through the eye of winter's star;
I know, you always loved the steel guitar
and once again you played for me. Moonlight
had barely filtered through my willow tree
across the pond. A robin had begun
her early tune beneath the eave, and one
small cloud along the crest had wrestled free
to dissipate above the water's sheen,
like wayward thoughts that move without a helm
or sail, to float upon another realm.
Your quiet song still resonates between
the sky and earth, for me. It dwells upon
lamenting clouds, then slides into the dawn.

Autumn Ambivalence

We sit near the stream edge, under the pine's
brittle fingers. Our collective breath
drapes between low branches

like a foggy sheet across autumn's arms.
You spot a black bear in the distance;
I marvel how a sky so blue

can be so cold. Daylight has become
brief, the valley blurred into a ribbon
of frayed leaves. At dusk I see

Denali's shadow from my balcony,
moose eat fuchsias by the backyard deck.
Stalks of rhubarb bend

and twist to earth, breathing
a chilly sigh. No matter how many
winters I greet, this place

will always seem foreign to me.
Everything lies exposed, the beauty
is too vast. God is too near.

Somewhere near Evesham

December swept the cemetery lawn;
the drone of church bells bridged the waterway.
On ancient tombstones, near the abbey wall,
each epitaph was faint and worn away.

But then that special one, in front of me,
had blossoms reaching upward from the ground,
all yellow, bright as spring. And when I read
the words engraved, a sleeping voice I found—

it softly echoed out in hope these words:
"Although my body is corrupt, I shall
again be whole." And all the way I thought
of her, while wandering the long canal.

Eyeball Prayer

I thank the Lord for marvelous eyes that
transform small piles of books upon my bench
into a multicolored June bouquet
of blooms, and hide long smudges on the French

doors every time the kitten rubs her paw
against the pane. For eyes that never see
clothes falling from a laundry basket, or
detect the chips on a piano key.

I thank the Lord for eyes that are unlike
my husband's—always rolling in dismay
at beds unmade, and going crossed when large
spoons mix with small, inside the kitchen tray.

Anywhere

Perhaps it was the somber vines between
those leaves, or how a moon spilled lavender
through parted sheers, and blended shades of green
against my wall, that made me think of her.

Or maybe, it was trusting mourning doves
who left their eggs behind when dawn imbued
a citrine sky. I know about her loves.
They echo in the beauty she pursued

like scents of hyacinth in June, or song
that fills a hillside church, and solemn prayer.
Each day I think: *it seems so very long
since I have sensed her presence, anywhere.*

Lament of the Leaves

I caught a maple leaf
within my palm. Its body
frail as parchment, pressed
with brittle veins—

just a tinge of gold remained,
like some intrinsic breath
garnered from a springtime ray.

I placed it down for sedges
to reclaim. They cradled it
until the snowflakes came.

Freedive

It was obvious from the large photos
framed in our family room—headshots of groupers, eels,
and sheepshead—that my father embraced the ocean.

Our bookshelves sported abalone shells
and a puffer fish dangling from a line. A large homemade
coffee table with cork legs and carved whale shapes
filled the middle of the room. Our screened porch
was draped in netting, woven wallpaper,
glass balls, and a pair of carved coconut heads.

We had no snapshots of kids swimming in Baja,
no pictures of mom sunbathing in Mazatlán.
Only the parrotfish tilted above the rustic mantel.

After dad passed on, his hard hat, weight belt,
rotting flippers, and regulator, were tossed away. He had hung
on to them for years, dreaming of his last undersea excursion.

In the hospital, he floated on a foam mattress
while an eternity of wavy lines rolled across the monitor.
Like a brilliant sunfish gaffed on the beach,
his color paled in increments.

He angled through his options.
He said he wanted to go home.
He said he wanted to go fast.

Then he removed his oxygen mask
and began a freedive.

On the British Riviera

We step across the green onto the promenade
and watch a sloop transition past the harbor of Torquay.
It's late afternoon. Beside me, a German woman
chatters about her retirement and relocation
to the city center. Her husband sleeps

in a hired deck chair, his yellow canvas hat
slanted across his face. Beside a long line of beach huts,
a mother rummages through her bag for coins
and sends her daughter to the ice cream stand.

I trace my finger over your skin, feeling
a raised line between the wrist and thumb—
the only evidence of your twenty-five year
racing career. Its faint glossiness has tattooed

you with your former self, a thin scar
from another era. We marvel at the lack
of waves and watch the sun wedge shadows
between rows of white Victorians
near the strand. Trees line the sidewalks

as easterly winds chicane through their fronds.
They remind me of old people, minds rustling
over a sea of yesterdays, waving at tourists
on the British Riviera—each with a story
ridged into their palm.

Hard Hat Diver

He keeps his diving helmet in a shed.
The memories that it buoys up, aren't dead—
that heavy hat of bolts protects his pride.
He seldom ever has to look inside
the wooden crate beneath the old work bench,
where all his man-things: chisel, hammer, wrench,
as if in dry dock, wait to be reused.
His wife told him to toss it, he refused.
You're eighty-five, you'll never need that thing!
But somehow, he can never seem to bring
himself to entertain the thought. The brass
is surely worth a fortune, and the glass …
The chance is slim, but yet he still regards
an abalone dive as in the cards.

Tides and Anchors

Beneath the pier, waves swirl in shades of daiquiri green,
like the ice cream I loved as a child—
my gritty hands shivering after a swim, tightly wrapped
around a brittle cone.

Along the jetty, calloused by winter winds, gulls tuck
in against the five o'clock breeze.
We interlace fingers and walk the promenade
where young boys beat plastic tubs and sing off-tune.

This time of day reminds you of England's
coastline. We come here often, shuffling in the same direction—
toward the shell shop, Tony's Bar, and the pearl store,
pausing to watch fishermen bait their hooks. At the pier's end,

I relax on a blue metal bench and listen to a buoy bell
while you fish change from your pockets to buy us both a churro,
careful to leave quarters left for the parking meter.

We had lost it all, back then, in a financial riptide
as we dogpaddled against the force of the recession.
We didn't know those glimpses of Catalina

at sunset, soft clicks of our flip flops on the boardwalk,
and the statuesque pelicans poised on the rails,
were our life preservers.

Seaside at Eighty

We'll breakfast at Las Brisas when we're gray,
discussing all our commonalities
and differences, admiring the breeze.
We'll idly chatter on about the way

long rocking eucalyptus branches seem
to hammock threads of morning sun along
the coast. Pale clouds will shift to butter-cream
and melon, swimming through a blue sarong

of tinctured sky. I'll scan the beach and sea
where I once played in tide pools as a child,
then you will say: *The waves are much more mild*
on Devon's shore, I really miss Torquay.

I'll point to where the beach-worn mussel shells
bloom purple, Catalina's outline might
appear beyond the shoals of blue-green swells.
We'll venture forth, oblivious to white

sails cutting southward, tilting toward the shore,
where we had often bathed and sunned before;
and like two cockle halves worn from the weather,
we'll linger by the oceanfront together.

Retired Breaststroke Swimmer Finds a Pool

Now once again I baptize every pore
in sunlit waters of the swimming pool,
immersed beneath the silence and the cool,
to move innately as I did before.

My body finds its lost propulsive motion;
each muscle lengthens in a surge and glide,
my forearms reach to circle semi-wide—
I breathe, I kick, releasing all emotion.

In you my hesitation disappears;
remake me supple, limber as a teen;
embrace and cloak me in your gauzy green:
this prodigal who's been away for years.

Parrotfish

Dad rose from the surf, called me,
and kicked off his fins. It twitched
in shallow water, still impaled
on the spear. Green and blue scales
glistened beneath a headdress of sea foam
until its body paled. Dad nailed
it to the patio wall by his diving treasures—
abalone shells, a puffer fish
that became a hanging lamp, glass balls
in nets, and his old diving helmet.
Only the parrotfish faced the pool.
I often thought how cruel
it had to watch us swim.

How to Break a Northern Spell

Remember your expensive basket
of fuchsias the moose ate before sun-up,
and the fat mosquitoes that hovered
around your head when the bedroom lights
went out. Recall how the kids stumbled off to school
each morning, beneath street lights
that barely lit the sidewalk. Count the hours
they wouldn't go to bed in summer
because the sun never left the sky.
Keep in mind the grubby snowsuits
you zipped and unzipped, so the children
could pee every two hours.
Think about the dog and his dirty
kennel, car locks that froze, the Chinook wind
that picked up your neighbor's balcony
and flung it into your yard. Erase the feel
of static electricity zapping your finger
every time you flicked a light switch.
Imagine the scent of a wet wool blazer.
Pack all those memories
into a tarnished little locket, rub it
like a counter-charm—then dig your toes
into the California sand.

Home Decor

I remember sunning on the sand—
my dad in wet-gear rising from the sea,
an air tank on his shoulders, like Godzilla,
throwing off his mask and calling me.
He dragged a mid-sized parrotfish he'd speared,
out of the foam. Its turquoise body flipped
against the beach. I noticed how in minutes
every scale turned ghostly grey, and slipped
from glorious to dull. The taxidermist
restored it to its brilliant, deep-blue self.
Above the sliding door we hung it just
for show. Along a full-length teakwood shelf,
we loaded gemmy doodads from the store.
That handsome fish was hatched for our decor.

Troubles, Curiosities, and Observations

A Californian Views British Soap Operas

The cast looks like they could be one of "us"
with baggy eyes and double chins. No fuss
to find a perfect "10" seems to exist.
I find it freeing, but there is a twist—

a culture war's exploding in my head.
The push to look amazing is widespread;
I've grown up where long legs and breasts abound
and women run themselves into the ground

financially—then wind up looking plastic.
But here in England, I'm a bit sarcastic.
I sit and watch the women on the shows,
note body types and non-designer clothes.

In judging my own kind I need a nurse;
these California values are a curse.

Compositions by the River Dee

At six o'clock we cross the fieldstone bridge,
descend the footpath to the River Dee;
with boots and brollies, moving comfortably,
traverse through sheep dung stippled near the ridge

to watch the sun abate before sky molds
into a pewter veil above our heads.
The cattle flatten out their clover beds,
long reeds reflect in water, dusk unfolds,

as solitude soothes lilies, oaks, wild leeks,
sheep congregate and snuggle for the night;
A single lamb limps near—his dismal plight
parades before our eyes. My husband speaks

"The farmer doesn't care." Then we concede
we're clueless about life's uncanny laws—
its roll-of-dice deficiencies, heaped flaws,
on innocents that only sleep and feed.

A Troubled Lot

As Lot engaged in supper, rowdy neighbors
disturbed his peaceful aura, shouting jeers;
he offered them his tender-minded daughters
(which gave them insecurities for years).

It didn't help at all they were rejected
by every guy who pounded on the door;
at sunrise they were ready to relocate
and gamble on what else could be in store.

They didn't realize they'd live in mountains,
and have no running water or a sink;
the evenings were a drag unless they pilfered
a swig of booze they saw their father drink.

The prospect of a husband was unheard of,
they put their heads together, formed a plot,
removed their nighties—slept with drunken daddy.
By winter two were added to the lot.

Superchild

Alone on the playground's edge,
surrounded by a troupe of invisible ballerinas
who transform her frayed skirt into a flash of tulle

while others play foursquare and hopscotch
on the blacktop, she exercises her superpowers
by blocking out thoughts of her mother's demons.

At night she crawls into bed, waking up alone
in the house at midnight—but nothing frightens her.
A swift cat scratch across her cheek imparts

no sting, she can hold back a decade of tears
with a single squint. Neighborhood children
never hear the words

that wrestle within her head, and even adults
struggle to see evidence of the mother's love
her x-ray vision barely captures.

Chain Stitch

My mother's sewing room has spools of thread
stored on a little wooden rack that's mounted
above her old machine—fifty-five pegs
filled with various colors (I have counted).

Long, loose ends dangle over one another,
frail generations crossing down the wall.
She always puts them back in place when finished:
each signifies a project, large or small,

made of those deeper jewel shades she loves.
And I, a pale blonde daughter, see light-blue
incorporated into her collection,
for pastel dresses, she made just a few

decades ago. The pink was for my prom
dress made of cotton taffeta, when nimble
fingers shaped my world, and taught me all
I needed was a pattern, cloth, and thimble.

Outlooks

He drank his booze and climbed the metal ladder
(they always argued savagely, those two).
The roof, his own Nirvana, made her madder
when he escaped, inventing jobs to do.
I often thought an ambulance was in
the cards, because of their unearthly shouts.
I wondered if their love had ever been
alive, or if their crazy, violent bouts
had killed it off, until the illness came.
It took away her speech, she couldn't walk
or feed herself. He hovered near, became
a different man, who whispered loving talk
into her ears; and never left her side
but once. (He went up on the roof and cried.)

The Drive

I'm riding in the backseat of the car.
The mountains lift their blue chemise of cloud,
while pre-dawn haze stirs quietly. Bizarre,
how palms along the roadside all look bowed
beneath the desert air. Last night it rained—
mesquites are yellow as a slice of sun.
My parents are in front—I'm self-contained,
my young mind on vacation, watching one
by one, as fresh-washed stars depart. It's been
near forty years since I've been in this seat.
I fold my hands, pretend I'm young again,
not heading to the hospital to meet
white gowns that blend and morph into each other.
My parents chatter on and I am blind
to fates that whirl and storm above my mother.
This morning I'm the girl time left behind.

Much from Little

She forms and threads small beads. At eighty-five,
nothing much else makes her come alive.
Bright paisley colors, shining crystals add
so much to any outfit. Once she had
a life of travel, now she drives to shop
a distance of just thirty miles, nonstop,
to pick through findings, swirly patterned papers.
When she gets home, she holds her needle, tapers
edges; wraps and pastes, then lacquers them
in imitation of a precious gem.
All time is tarnished, only gradual changes
occur as endless bead work re-arranges.
To leave with us some talent she would save
for gem encrusted garlands for her grave.

Summer in Italy

It's been two days since
your chemo session.

We lie together on the bed,
mother and daughter, sinking into
a mattress of memory foam.

Furniture is familiar in this room—
your teak dresser is forty years old,
and the green lamp still
mushrooms above the end table.
A Mediterranean scene

accents the wall. White sails
splash against summer-blue, terraced homes
rise in the foreground. Two women
link arms by the sea.
You whisper, *I wish I was there.*

Pastoral for the Midlands

The heart-shaped linden leaves have netted veins
that web into a rib along their center;
the blades are broad with scalloped edges, catching
October's sun, as filmy light rays enter

between strong layered branches. By the Severn,
we walk the well-worn, narrow bridleways.
Our trail is trimmed in sedges, maples drop
their dappled leaves in paper-thin arrays,

to fan the feet of ancient brambles. Roots
rise from a hidden ditch; the sun burns off
earth's rim of mist; a patch of peacock blue
appears above a whitewashed mill. Clouds doff

in salutation to the sky. The bleats
of farmland sheep float through the country air.
The valley steam train lets its whistle out
as we rest by the waters of the weir.

This place is far from what I'm used to. Thick
with large leaved limes and sycamores . . . My home
is scorching desert and mesquite, stretched suns
like ribbons dipped in scarlet strands that comb

through warm horizons. But lush emerald hues,
medieval bridges, plentitudes of calm,
no sand dune is superior to these.
The blends of meadow-breeze, the water's balm,

brushstrokes of nature, delicate as sorrel,
create a shady mural for my mind.
And there I find the time to pause, reflect,
when the harshness of the desert seems unkind.

Tumbleweed

We are the village, and you are the child
whose mother cares for the senile
man, across the way, filling his spare

beds with strung-out strangers.
Tumbleweed-girl, with wind-blown hair,
you roll from one neighbor's house to another.

We dress you in pinafores and tie bows
around your pigtails, take you to museums
and ballets, knock on your window

to wake you for school. We feed
you French toast and buy you glittery
barrettes. We are the village,

surrounding the only spark of life
left in a house so crammed with living dead,
no one can see the emptiness.

Remnants

It's such a shame to see the flowers finished,
their blossoms strewn in disarray. All beauty
once tenderly maintained is now diminished,
and caring for it has become a duty.

Forget-me-nots I've pressed and dried in pages
watch daisies turn to dust after decay.
For each and every thing evolves in stages,
comes springing up in its due time. Today

I'll search for bulbs once more, reject each stone
between dead stems, wild briar. I'll cradle clay
that knows my touch, my voice, my every bone
and waits for me to name the time I'll stay.

Lady of Shalott

French tapestries, embroidered with spun gold,
hang down against your polished cherry walls.
Around sachets of lavender you fold
soft skeins of yarn. A distant tower calls.
You pause to hear Westminster chimes—a song
that's carried up from Camelot. Light weaves
with shadow near the window pane. A long
alluring ray gleams through the barley sheaves.
Your dress is caught beneath the chair and rips.
You brace yourself to stop the fall, and wield
the loom against the mirror. Your world tips,
dismantled by a knight across the field.
The canvas is in ruins, you're distraught,
and no one else is left but Lancelot.

In the Smoky Mountains

She was an orchid by a mountain pass,
along an Appalachian trail of blue.
He was a hemlock near the cotton grass,
with crooked branches, needles, limbs askew.
At twilight, they'd admire the dazzling way
celestial bodies filled the void with sparks,
both disillusioned by the glaring day,
unsatisfied with melodies of larks.
She wrapped her leaves around his trunk until
they grew together, some say it was fate.
He kept her shaded for a summer, till
the sky became too heavy of a weight.
By autumn, vines and roots joined in a wreath,
that dried with broken pine cones underneath.

Surprise Possession

She spends her afternoons beside the tree,
where Mr. Lizard's made his home. Last week
she caught him in her mouth, and forcefully,
my husband pried him out. She doesn't seek
this reptile, or a patterned, scaly prize—
just itches for a thrilling chase. For days
she's turned into a sphinx. Unblinking eyes,
and breath held in her breast. Her mind's ablaze
with thoughts of how he was in her possession.
He watches from the wall where he's protected.
They play their waiting game. No intercession
at dusk is needed. She comes inside dejected,
and marches to the house to scheme and plot.
Tomorrow she will have another shot.

Needlepoint in Blue

Here comes the cold time, holly, pine, and yew,
low grass-laced hills crisscross in winter white;
dark threads of cloud stretch sugar-plum and blue
along a canvas sky of fraying light.

The frost arranges crystals on a limb.
Flakes, falling, reappear as snow on snow
like French knots sewn above the tree root's rim,
that stencil little patterns, to and fro.

The frozen oak is filled with mistletoe,
its yellow berries unconcealed by leaf.
They offer fruit for robin, thrush, and crow.
It makes me think of emptiness and grief,

reminds me of a summer field of yarrow,
and everything that bloomed before the chill.
December brings a tapestry of sorrow,
with knots pulled through a surface of goodwill.

Away from the Care Center

Two upper teeth protrude
when he smiles. His receding hair
is turning gray, the color

of his almond-shaped eyes.
Only the shrillest sounds can enter his ears,
clunky eye glasses slide

down his nose. He unfolds
his napkin the way he was taught
as a child, slowly

and methodically. Over utensils,
hands pause politely by the plate,
his grin broadens; teeth dart out.

This is *his time* to choose
the food he eats and how many
helpings fill the dish,

escaping into a merry world of lemon
pudding, roast beef and ice cream.
There is no conversation—

only an occasional
thumbs up between bites.

Creating a Pastoral Scene

A turning point—
like a needle piercing a canvas,
pushing up from the blind underside
to revisit the world.

With each small tug
a thread appears, connecting
a row of holes that align
like silent days.

Today, I work in a field of blue,
blending small patches of sky
around trees, struggling
to find the pattern between hills and clouds,
heaven and earth.

Evil Eye

It's back again, the stupid dove,
the one Mom really resents
for nesting in her potted lantana
and flattening all the flowers.

This year, Mom hid the plant
and the bird settled in an empty
bucket on the balcony, boldly announcing
its arrival with flutters and coos.

After months of monopolizing
the corner, for its last egg never hatched,
Dad dared Mom to snatch
the egg during the dove's evening flight,

dye it for Easter, then slip
it back into the nest. But the dove
gave them such a nasty look before leaving,
Mom chickened out.

In a Hat Box

When I wake at three in the morning with stars
sprinkled between my curtains, and see
my old hat box wedged on the corner shelf
beneath scalloped shadows, I remember

its contents of unused wool from a needlepoint
canvas, colored pencils and the camera
with a broken lens. I recall a length of ribbon
too dark for my hair, business cards

that no longer matter, a plastic harmonica
from an amusement hall and an old monogrammed
handkerchief wrapped around a black and white
picture of you, leaning against a palm tree.

Back then, you were a transplanted Nebraskan
collecting San Diego summers in your pockets,
exploring tide pools and sailboats. Each Saturday
you rode the bus to Hotel Del Coronado

where big band music filled the Victorian ballroom.
One night you posed on the lawn in pearls and heels,
beneath a sand dollar moon embedded above the bay.
That was before you married dad. Before trips

to Bermuda and Europe, mundane chores, diapers,
three children, bike rides and sewing classes.
Before illness. When a slice of moon could move
across Coronado Bay and still glint in your eyes.

Kissing Gate

A partial sun suffuses slender weeds
in ocher light. Beside an echelon
of gorse and heather, wispy Maiden Pink
has nearly lost its bloom. The lapwing's gone

to glide across the mound and mind her young,
as silently as August slips away.
Long sedges with their tawny oval heads
spring out from brambles, forming a bouquet

of summer's final hues. Beyond the gate
a grassy hill has leveled out, it brings
a voiceless greeting to the lake. Here, dusk
meets treeless moor beneath a merlin's wings.

La Sierra 1946

I've come to reminisce, retracing all
your steps, beneath the symmetry of pines
and palms that colonnade near Angwin Hall.
The old rectangle chapel face aligns

its sacramental windows with the hills,
where sixty-years ago, inside those white
washed plaster walls your faith was found. Shade spills
like balm against the beveled glass. This fight,

to capture every yesteryear you've owned,
leaves me undone. The dormitory stairs
of walnut, tap an ageless chant—intoned
with all your giddy dreams and school-girl prayers.

The thought of you remains an oblique ray
of fleshless gold that burns my hours away.

On Hill Street

You settle into your old leather chair
against the dirty stucco wall, under a rotting
canopy. The bottle-strewn sidewalk rolls out
like a ketchup stained spreadsheet.
A white mug is balanced on your knee.

Every Thursday, I walk past you and trade
my dollar for your toothless smile.
We are not the same, my friend,
placed in our perspective office chairs.

All you own is folded into a rusty cart;
no complaints cling to your cracked lips.

You call me "your angel" as I slide
my money into the chipped cup.
I know you flatter me so I will return
next week. I flatter myself, too,
that I'm becoming more compassionate.

Leaving Alaska

I smile between thoughts
of tinkling ice cream carts and harbor bells,
while I pack for California.

Here, rhubarb is still on the ground,
frost is threatening pumpkin
and squash, my hated cross-country skis

have been tossed, along with Pendleton skirts.
I've said my good byes to rows of floatplanes,
the mint-blue inlet, and Talkeetna Range

where autumn-streaked valleys will never
find my footprints, or remember my name.

An Expatriate's Message

Remember me to homeland winter skies,
where dusk sifts purple ribbons through the leaves
around the linnets huddled in the limbs
of sycamores. Remember me to seas

and fishing villages between the bluffs,
cathedral bells and heather on the moor.
Recite my name when tufted mallards pass
beneath the bridge, and kindly reassure

the harebells they are missed. To thistle, woad,
valerian, extend regretful smiles.
This California sun has held me back
with bindweed grip, and bars me from the Isles.

Atomic Tiki Man

He's the one who looks
like he came from Trader Vic's,
wearing a sideways rum punch smile.
A cool dude who wants
to smooch long haired beachy girls
sipping coconut milk
under palm fronds.
His shirt is splashed with ruby
flowers that echo a suburban
shangri-la chair cushion. His hair
is an hibachi of charcoal curls.
It would take two hands
to wrap around those arms—
all tan and bendy
like a piece of rattan
(not the cheap wicker stuff).
His breath is scented
with passion fruit and pineapple.
At night he dines on crab rangoon
and sips Tiki Punch—then dreams
about taking a little wahine
with a purple orchid in her hair
on a tiki tour.

Sergeant Mockingbird

Between the green and gold brocade of branches,
a mockingbird explores his domicile.
In pale-lit morning of the frayed magnolia
he fans his wing-tips, checks the rank and file

through balustrades and portholes made of twigs.
He eyes the tabby on the wall, takes notes
on where the young retriever sleeps. The flick
and quirk of every sparrow wing denotes

a change of circumstance. He is aware
of his superiority. The cat
looks up as if to say, you are the Sergeant.
Clouds and clotheslines, little flies and gnats

report for duty as he squawks and scans
his daily list of rudimentary plans.

The Courtship Hour

I love the hour that hangs its weightless haze
of yawn across my bed. An ivory wrap
of humming stillness, spectral dance embossed
in thimble-light. I love the wentletrap

of thoughts and gurgled chants that twist before
white shoals of sleep. The bend and blur of night
with loveliness and brokenness inside
soft vagaries that pivot in the light.

I love the hour subservient to dreams,
when day's satiety leaves remnant sky,
and all beheaded moments shed their wings
into a hushed reluctance as they die.

The Old Racer

When the Tourist Trophy race
begins each year, he morphs
into his favorite chair
and turns on the telly.

Holding armrest handles
complete with imaginary helmet
and gloves, his glossy-eyed,
demonic expression reappears.

He calls out each bend and turn by name:
Bray Hill, Union Mills—a left-right hander,
Governors Bridge...

Fans cheer him on at each turn,
photo shoots await him, girls gather
for his autograph.

Then up the pub with his mates
for a pint of Guinness.

Like old helmet foam and a pair
of rotting leathers, his legacy
crumbles more each year.

No one would ever recognize him,
but for the wild look that dashes
from the depths of his easy chair.

At Sunset by the Oak

I've come into the shadow of the oak
to feel the spine of summer leaves. I've come
to rest in realms of dampness, darkness. Stroke
familiar branches beneath twilight's thumb.
I've come to wrap long vines around my breasts
and smear wet clay upon my dress. To weep.
The nutmeg colored bark becomes a test.
I find my way, I find my way. Time sweeps
me like a leaf across a fieldstone wall,
where like some flightless young, I huddle, cold.
I've never found forgiveness in the small
of night. That human element, controlled
by drifts of tulips and the lilacs' white.
That place I cannot love you in the light.

Drawing in the Sheets

And now, my parents' lives have come to this:
they've taken separate beds. At eighty-four,
my mother's moved into the extra room.
Her dresses line the closet, every drawer

is filled. They've lost their battle with the toss
and turn, the irritating reading light
that singed long shadows into dawn, and all
the sighs of each arthritic night.

A quiet harbinger of change lurks in
the hall, and scribbles words: *Alone, alone—*
and now they heed them following the lines,
before the fates interpret on their own.

When Autumn's Through

I cannot kick a mound of maple leaves
or see a pumpkin peeking from the vine
before the frost and not remember hills
where summer laid her green. A distant line

of poplars gleams like curtains made of coins;
it shakes at passing clouds. And everywhere
the magpie hops, I see another sign
of hawthorns beckoning the winter air

to breathe upon the fields. It once was mine,
that sweet transition only autumn knows,
the one that holds the oak limbs silently,
embracing every chilly breeze that blows.

It leads me into mottled shadows of
a deeper hue, where nothing seems so true
as winter's birth. Sometimes, I catch a glimpse
of it beneath the vines, when autumn's through.

Winter Widow

In Coeur d'Alene a red-hued sun has sketched
a portrait of the willows by the lake.
I watch her cut the last remaining rose
before the frost. Her hand picks up a rake

and lets it play one garden song, a dirge
of dying yellow. October glides away
like eagles on a cloudy afternoon
that dive into the chill of Mica Bay.

Her pears and apples have been gathered up
and brought into the kitchen. Soon the snow
will cover every hill. She folds her gloves,
remembering her daughters, long ago

this farmhouse had a family. Now deer
become her children, blending in the mire
of tawny dreams and cherry blossom springs.
She shuts the door and huddles by the fire.

Quiet Flame

I read through my old diary tonight.
Inside a sweater drawer is where I found
it, tattered travel log. It had a slight
tear on the spine, but still was neatly bound.
I reread all my thoughts throughout the night,
stone turrets wrapped in ivy, summer-crowned
green willow trees with soft Parisian light
across the way. My memory swirled around
each consecrated word, until your name
appeared, a shining brilliance so profound
it burnt the yellowed page with quiet flame.

Mariana

With lowing of the oxen, you will wake,
and like a crow that's ferried by the moon
across a changeless night into opaque
portholes of sky, your mind is strewn
inside the molding weeds and brambles
of the past. Your farmhouse leans aslant
with age, an edifice that sadly ambles
out an addle-minded creaky chant,
that taints the sparrow-song. Your moated grange,
where even Angelo was overcome
by fields of melancholy, dies. How strange
that dogtooth violets never bloom, and plum
trees wither markedly, their fruit askew
and dim. Depression always follows you.

Draining the Cup

After she agonized about the equity
disappearing from her home, and walking away
from the city where she grew up; after she wept
at the thought of leaving white plantation shutters
that slit the morning into little ribbons
of warmth, and the fireplace mantle she had constructed
to look like a picture in a magazine—

after she anguished over living in a small apartment
with no garden; after she announced she was taking her piano
with her, no matter what; after she talked to lawyers
and accountants who said there was no logic
in staying—

after she moved into a pint-sized rental
by the beach, and stopped the three-hour commute
each day; after she realized a dishwasher for two
wasted more time than it was worth; after she discovered
her cats got along better in a tiny area; after she could
sleep in, and have an extra cup of tea
before eight o'clock—

after she had no flowers to clip or sidewalks
to sweep; after she spent an hour on the sand and studied
a strip of scarlet cloud that stretched
from Palos Verdes to Santa Monica; after porpoise
appeared and the sun's back-glow turned the bay
into a goblet of rose-colored waves; after she bought
a hot chocolate on the pier and proclaimed it
the best dessert in the world—

she realized how delicious it could be
when the cup is drained.

Gathering Moss

You always stopped for no apparent reason,
whenever we walked into town, it drove
me crazy. Every slightest change in season
you'd find a little coppice in the grove,
or see a beetle laboring across
a fallen leaf. I had to break my pace,
transform into a stone that gathered moss.
I couldn't keep annoyance off my face.
And then my knee decided I should learn
to stroll with leisure, letting pain be teacher.
I spotted lilies, pale asparagus fern,
looked up to see the pear tree's every feature.
A faster stride? It almost seems unholy.
How glad I am you still like walking slowly.

Solace from a Pasture Gate

Old farm gate, flanked by rocks and hemmed in teasel,
where goldfinch garner seeds when weather's kind;
you yoke an ancient span of drystone walling
that keeps defenseless sheep and lambs confined.

One hundred years, your rails still firm and solid;
the latch lifts with a low arthritic cry;
it's cradled by rough lichen-covered fieldstones,
like clumsy crib rods, stable, yet awry.

You know the red kite, daisy, common mouse,
all nature, from the lowly to the grand;
your timber arm affirms that all is well
and balanced in this swath of pastureland.

British Guy

He has lived with that Californian
for twenty-six-years; the one who still tries
to microwave tea behind his back,
to see if he'll notice the difference.

She rolls her eyes when he refuses
to eat dinner and dessert using the same fork,
and still holds her breath while spreading
Marmite on his toast.

In the summertime
she forgets and adds ice cubes to his beverages
(then fishes them out with her fingers).
She says fried bread is disgusting.

Two decades have gone by, and still,
Branston Pickle has never touched her lips.
If it weren't for the way
she adores his accent, he'd be long gone.

Time Bomb

He once lived in a private subdivision.
Brooks Brothers, starched white shirts, pious donations,
expensive chairs and rugs, lined in precision,
were witness to the screams of his frustrations.

He snorted coke in increments all day;
his moods were an erratic pendulum.
At times, his wife would steal herself away,
to pop a pill or take a swig of rum.

She soothed herself with little shopping sprees.
Five years of this, their marriage hit the skids.
And still, much later on, his driven fears
rained down, like psychic shrapnel, on his kids

The Tortoise and the Hare

It's difficult to figure who'll go first;
mom, with her heart attack, pinched nerve and hip
that wakes her in the night, the chemo drip
still in her veins, or dad, his mass submersed

in slothfulness, who might conceivably
sit in his chair and sink into a coma,
unnoticed, till the dinnertime aroma
would cease to wake him (unbelievably).

My mother swims ten laps a day, hell-bound
to ride her bike at eighty-five. She walks
and chatters constantly. Father seldom talks,
embellishes dessert with cream. The ground

moans beneath his widening girth. My mom
is trim and neat, her sewing room's in order;
dad's office looks like he's a first-class hoarder.
The winning post waits like an atom bomb,

or unseen trophy in the 4th dimension.
My father sitting on the couch, no stress,
and mother cooking in her Sunday dress.
I watch the finish line with apprehension.

Drama in the Garden

Within my rosebush, when I thought to check
the welfare of finch nestlings, I discovered
an emptied bowl of twigs with nothing left.
The parents, stunned and flitting nearby, hovered

just below the neighbor's broad mesquite.
The family seemed brilliantly secluded,
beneath sharp thorns and leaves that camouflaged
their small retreat; the parents had eluded

my cat (although they tolerated me,
if my chair was not positioned near).
Each morning I spent checking up on them.
I'd wait until I thought the coast was clear,

and reach my arm in for a photograph:
Four beaks wide open, in a patch of light,
a bit of fluff around small brown-tipped wings.
I'd speculate on their initial flight.

But then they vanished quickly as they came,
without a hint of who, or what to blame.

Winter in England

It's here I pause with each December, where
the snow trimmed walls of timeworn brick align
beneath the window sill, and winter's bare
limbs bend beneath a delicate and fine

glossing of frost. It's here I garner all
my thoughts of months gone past, beside the sheers
and yellow paisley chair. A woolen shawl,
a pearl and knit of smiles and raveled tears,

is wrapped around my shoulders. Nothing speaks
but morning's melting icicles, and wind
that steals the breath of graying skies. The creek
is frozen into timelessness and thinned

with dying grasses, every shade of brown.
I take my stock of daisies dried and pressed,
my verses, scratched impetuously down—
time balanced here on its mid-point of rest.

About the Author

Karen Kelsay is the editor for the online poetry journal, *The Orchards*. She also owns Kelsay Books, a rapidly growing poetry publishing company. Karen's poems have been printed in a variety of formalist and free verse journals. She has authored several books and chapbooks: *Lavender Song* (Fortunate Childe Publications 2011), *In Spite of Her* (Flutter Press 2010), *Song of the Bluebell Fairy* (Pudding House Publications 2010), *A Fist of Roots* (Pudding House Publications 2009), *Somewhere Near Evesham* (The New Formalist 2009), and two full length collections, *Dove on a Church Bench* (Punkin House 2011), and *Amytis Leaves Her Garden* (White Violet Press 2012).

Karen has been published in numerous anthologies, including *Fire in the Pasture* (Peculiar Pages 2011) a collection of 21st century Mormon poets. In 2012, she received the Fluvanna Award from *The Lyric,* and the Association For Mormon Letters Award for her full-length poetry book *Amytis Leaves Her Garden.* She is a six-time Pushcart Prize nominee and has been the featured poet in many magazines including: *The Nervous Breakdown,* Russell Bittner's *Poet's Corner, Kin Poetry Journal, A Motley Vision, Thick with Conviction* and *The HyperTexts.* Her picture and biography may be found at The Poetry Foundation's website and at her personal website: Karenkelsay.com

Made in the USA
San Bernardino, CA
26 January 2018